DO NOT BE AFRAID

Bible Stories for Kids about Hope

JARED DEES

_____

For more information visit jareddees.com.

Paperback: ISBN 978-1-7332048-4-2
eBook: ISBN 978-1-7332048-5-9

First Edition

CONTENTS

INTRODUCTION

"O Israel, hope in the Lord! For with the Lord there is stead-fast love, and with him is great power to redeem."

Psalm 130:7

Hope is the desire for happiness combined with the trust that God will provide for us. As Christians we place our hope in the Lord and look forward to the happiness of the kingdom of heaven.

Hope is hard when you feel alone. But you are not alone. God is here. He is with you. He has sent others to be with you in times of need, just as he will send you to others when they are in need of a little hope.

Every one of us will go through times in our lives that seem hopeless. The dreams we have may seem impossible. Challenges will stand before us. Do we give up? Do we despair? Do we wait in fear? Place your hope in the Lord who loves you, and he will give you peace.

At other times, we will face challenges that put fear into our hearts. We may not be hopeless, but we can sense there is fear holding us back. How do we get past that fear? Turn to God. Place your hope in the Lord.

The Bible contains many stories of people who felt hopeless. They came to the brink of doubt, but God gave them assurance to maintain trust in him. They had hope because they had faith. This is the one constant theme in every one of the stories you will read in this book. Do you want to find happiness and freedom from fear? Trust in God. Have faith in him that he will provide for you.

The many stories about hope contained in this collection culminate in the greatest story: Jesus died and rose again so that we could rise with him, too. He gives us hope. He gives us peace. He stirs within us a longing for the love that will erase all doubts.

It is my great joy to share with you these stories of hope from the Old and New Testament. I hope they will be a light for you in times when you are troubled. May they inspire you to overcome any fear you might have, no matter how big or small. Have faith in God. Place your hope in the Lord.

"Faith is the assurance of things hoped for, the conviction of things not seen."

Hebrews 11:1

NOAH AND THE FLOOD

Genesis 6-9

Long ago, the world was filled with very sinful people. God decided to punish them. Noah was a good man. God called him to gather his family and two of every animal into his large boat (the ark) while the earth was flooded.

As you read this story, pay attention to the promise God makes to Noah after the flood.

Once Noah had loaded the last pair of animals onto his ark, the rain came down and the water started to rise. The flood was so great that the water rose high above the mountains.

Only Noah, his family, and the many animals in their care remained, floating above the water on the ark during the forty days of rain. It felt like a very long time. Noah continued to trust in God with hope that the flood would soon end.

Then God finally sent the wind to settle the waters.

The flood subsided. The ark settled on top of a mountain.

Noah opened up a window and looked out over the earth. He sent a dove to make sure the flood was completely ended. The dove came back holding a branch from an olive tree. Noah knew the world was at peace again.

God made a promise to Noah never to flood the earth again. To show that promise, God sent a rainbow as another sign of peace. The rainbows that come after rain are a sign that God will not punish the whole earth again with a flood.

REFLECTION QUESTIONS

What promise did God give to Noah after the flood?

What makes you feel peaceful, like the dove and the rainbow in this story?

How can you bring peace to the people around you?

A SON FOR ABRAHAM AND SARAH

Genesis 18–19

God promised Abraham and Sarah that they would have many descendants, but they grew very old and still were unable to have children together. They thought it would be impossible to have children now that they were old, but God maintained his promise that they would have a son and name him Isaac.

As you read this story, pay attention to Sarah's reaction when the angels promise that she will have a son.

Abraham sat outside his tent in the middle of a hot day. All of a sudden, he was surprised to see three men standing near him. Although he did not know it at the time, the men were angels in disguise. He got up quickly to greet them.

He said to them, "My lord, if I find favor with you, do not pass by your servant. Let me give you a little water and wash your feet so that you can rest yourselves under a tree. Let me bring you some bread, too, before you go."

"Do as you have said," they replied.

Abraham ran into the tent to Sarah and asked her to prepare three loaves of bread for them. Then he went out to ask a servant to prepare some meat for them, as well. He brought all these things for them to eat.

"Where is your wife Sarah?" they asked.

"There, in the tent," Abraham replied.

One of them said, "I will return to you next year, and your wife Sarah shall have a son."

Sarah overheard this from the entrance of the tent. She had longed for a son for many years but had never been able to have a baby. She was very old by this time and could not contain her laughter.

Then they said to Abraham, "Why did Sarah laugh? Is there anything too wonderful for the Lord? Sarah shall have a son."

The Lord did as he promised for the couple. Sarah conceived and bore Abraham a son. They named him Isaac, which means "laughter."

When her son was born, Sarah said, "God has brought laughter for me; everyone who hears will laugh with me. Who would have ever said that we would have children? Yet I have given birth to a son in my old age."

REFLECTION QUESTIONS

Why did Sarah laugh when she heard the angels say she would give birth to a son?

Has anything ever happened to you that made you laugh?

How can you laugh about life like Sarah did in this story?

JOSEPH THE DREAMER

Genesis 37–50

Joseph, the son of the Patriarch Jacob, was sold into slavery by his jealous brothers, but God had a plan for him. God turned a sad situation into a miracle that saved many lives.

As you read this story, pay attention to the reason Joseph so easily forgives his brothers.

After being betrayed by his brothers, Joseph was taken into Egypt and then thrown in jail for a crime he did not commit. In jail, he sometimes felt discouraged, but through his faith, he became known as someone who could interpret dreams. So when Pharaoh, the king of Egypt, was having sleepless nights full of difficult dreams, he summoned Joseph from jail.

"I have had a dream, and no one can interpret it. But I am told you have the ability to interpret dreams," Pharaoh said to Joseph.

"It is not me. God will give you an answer to your dreams," Joseph replied.

Pharaoh described his dream, and Joseph explained to him that it meant the next seven years would bring a great harvest, with lots of food. The seven years after that, however, would bring a famine, with very little food.

Pharaoh was impressed. He appointed Joseph to oversee the kingdom to prepare for the famine. Joseph became one of the most powerful men in the world.

Seven years later, Joseph's family in Canaan was suffering from the famine. They were very hungry. His brothers traveled down to Egypt to ask for help. They did not know that their brother Joseph had become such an important person.

They appeared before Joseph to ask for Egypt's help, but they did not recognize him as their brother. Joseph, however, recognized them. He tested them to see if they had changed, and indeed, they had. He revealed to them that he was their brother Joseph, and they were filled with remorse.

They worried that Joseph would hold a grudge against them. They asked for his forgiveness.

Joseph wept when he heard this, and his brothers wept, too, and bowed down before Joseph, saying, "We are here as your slaves!"

Joseph replied, "Do not be afraid! Am I in the place of God? You intended to do me harm, but God intended it for good. I was brought here so he could save many people. Have no fear. I will provide for you and for your children in Egypt."

So the people of God traveled to Egypt and lived there through the famine and for many years afterward.

REFLECTION QUESTIONS

Why did Joseph so easily forgive his brothers instead of holding a grudge or punishing them?

How might this story give hope to someone in a difficult situation?

Have you ever had a memorable dream? What happened in the dream, and what do you think it means?

MOSES AND THE BURNING BUSH

Exodus 3; 4:10-17

Joseph protected the Israelites in Egypt, but after many generations, the Israelites became slaves to the Egyptians. God sent Moses to help free the Israelites and lead them back to the promised land of Canaan. When God called Moses, however, the man had doubts that he could be the one to bring hope to the people of Israel.

As you read this story, pay attention to the reasons God gives for Moses to have confidence in himself.

Moses was watching over a flock of sheep at the foot of a mountain. Suddenly, a bush nearby burst into flames. The bush was on fire, but the branches did not burn up. The fire did not destroy the bush.

"I must look to see why this bush is blazing but not burned up," he said.

Then God called Moses from the bush and said, "Moses, Moses!"

"Here I am," Moses replied.

"Do not come any closer! Take off your sandals, for you are standing on holy ground," said God.

Moses did as he was commanded.

"I am the God of your father, the God of Abraham, the God of Isaac, and the God of Jacob," the Lord said from the bush.

Moses hid his face, for he was afraid to look at God.

The Lord said, "I have seen the sadness of my people in Egypt. I have heard their cries. I know their sufferings. I have come down to lead them out of Egypt and into the good land that I promised to them."

Moses could hardly believe God was speaking to him. Only a short time ago, he had been cast out of Egypt. His heart ached for the suffering of the people who remained there without him.

Then God said, "I will send you to Pharaoh to bring my people, the Israelites, out of Egypt."

Moses replied, "Who am I that I should go to Pharaoh and bring the Israelites out of Egypt?"

God said, "I will be with you."

But Moses was still unsure. "If I come to the Israelites and say, 'God sent me to you,' and they ask me, 'What is his name?' what shall I tell them?"

God said, "I am who I am. Say to the Israelites, 'I AM has sent me to you.'"

Before Moses could object again, God said, "The Israelites will listen to you. You will also go to Pharaoh, but he will not let my people go until he sees the wonders that I will perform. Then he will let them go."

Moses said, "But, Lord, I have never been good at speaking. People have a hard time understanding me."

"Who gives the ability to speak to people? Who makes them deaf or blind? Is it not I, the Lord? Now go, and I will be your mouth and teach you what you are to speak."

But Moses was still afraid, and he persisted, "Oh, please, send someone else!"

God was angry with Moses for his many objections, but he said, "Your brother Aaron speaks fluently. You shall speak to him. I will be with your mouth and with his mouth, and I will teach you what you shall do."

This made Moses feel better, but God had one more gift for him. "Take with you your staff, for I will work many miracles through it for signs to convince Pharaoh to release my people."

Moses left that holy place and returned to Egypt, where by the power of God he was able to free his people.

REFLECTION QUESTIONS

Why did Moses have doubts in his ability to free the people? How did God promise to help him?

Who are the family and friends that help you when you need it most, just as Aaron helped Moses?

What items do you own in your bedroom or in your house that can give you hope, just as the staff of Moses gave him hope?

CROSSING THE RED SEA

Exodus 14

After God performed many miracles, Pharaoh finally released the Israelites from Egypt. Moses led the people out into the wilderness, but then Pharaoh changed his mind and came after the Israelites with his army.

As you read this story, pay attention to what God says and does for the Israelites to save them.

Pharaoh gathered all the chariots in Egypt to chase after the Israelites and bring them back as slaves again. Even Pharaoh mounted his chariot and set out for the Israelite camp.

From far away, the Israelites could see Pharaoh and his army coming for them. They were struck with fear and cried out to the Lord.

They turned to Moses and said, "Have you brought us here to die in the wilderness? What have you done to us? It would have been better for us to stay as slaves in Egypt than die out here alone!"

Moses said to the people, "Do not be afraid. Stand firm and see what the Lord will accomplish for you today. He will fight for you. Just keep still."

Then the Lord said to Moses, "Why do you cry out to me? Lift up your staff, and stretch out your hand over the sea to divide it. Tell the Israelites to go forward and walk through the middle of the sea on the dry ground. The Egyptians will follow and know that I am the Lord."

Then an angel of God went before the Israelites to lead them. A cloud formed between the Egyptians and the Israelites.

Moses stretched out his hand, and a strong wind created a path of dry land through the sea, with walls of water on both sides. The Israelites traveled through the sea safely to the other side.

The Egyptians followed them through the parted waters, but the wheels of their chariots became clogged in the mud. Moses stretched out his hand again so that the water would crash over the Egyptians.

The Israelites saw the great work of the Lord and how he saved them from the Egyptians. They saw this and believed in the Lord and in his servant Moses.

REFLECTION QUESTIONS

What complaint did the Israelites make to Moses?

How did God save them from the Egyptians?

What are you most afraid of right now? How can you ask God to help you overcome this fear?

RUTH AND NAOMI

Ruth 1

Ruth was the great-grandmother of King David, but she was born as a foreigner in the country of Moab. It was Ruth's dedication to her mother-in-law, Naomi, even after her husband had died, that led her into the land of Israel.

As you read this story, pay attention to how loyal Ruth is to Naomi in her time of need.

Naomi and her husband had two sons. Both sons married women from another country called Moab. The women's names were Ruth and Orpah.

Sadly, Naomi's husband died before their sons were married. Ten years later, her sons also died. All three women were now alone.

Naomi said to her daughters-in-law, "Go back to your homes and your families. May the Lord God treat you as kindly as you have treated me. May the Lord give you security and houses with new husbands."

She kissed them both and then wept.

"No, we will return with you to your people," they said.

"Turn back, my daughters! Why would you go with me? I will have no more sons to give to you as husbands, and I am too old to take another husband myself," she told them.

She paused and said sadly, "The Lord has turned against me."

All three women wept aloud. Then Orpah kissed her mother-in-law and left to return to Moab. Ruth, however, stayed and hugged Naomi in her tears.

Naomi said, "Orpah has gone back to her people and to her gods. Go and return with her to Moab."

"Do not turn me away from following you!" Ruth replied. "Wherever you go, I will go. Wherever you live, I will live. Your people shall be my people, and your God will be my God."

Naomi saw that Ruth was determined to stay with her so that she would not be alone. She said no more, and the two of them left for Bethlehem to live among the people of God.

REFLECTION QUESTIONS

What did Ruth promise to do for Naomi when her mother-in-law tried to send her away?

Who would be there for you if you were in a difficult time or lost someone you loved?

How can you comfort friends or family members who are in times of need?

DAVID DEFEATS GOLIATH

1 Samuel 17

Goliath was a great and powerful warrior for the Philistine enemies of Israel. No one could defeat him in battle, and the entire Israelite army was afraid of him.

As you read this story, pay attention to the reasons David has confidence and hope that he will be able to defeat Goliath.

The Israelites were at war with the Philistines. They gathered together and prepared on both sides for battle. But before the two armies could fight, a great warrior named Goliath came out to challenge the Israelites.

He wore a bronze helmet and a strong coat of chain-mail armor. He had a great sword and spear, as well as a shield for battle. He shouted toward the Israelite camp, "Choose a man for yourselves to fight me. If he is able to kill me, then the Philistines will be your servants. But if I defeat him, you shall serve us!"

There was no answer, so Goliath shouted louder, "Give me a man, that we may fight together!"

King Saul of Israel was very afraid. No one in his army was brave enough to fight such a great warrior. Outside of the camp, however, there was a young man named David. David was a shepherd and was supposed to be too young to fight in the war. His father had sent him with food to give to his older brothers, who were on the front lines of the army.

David arrived just as his brothers and the other soldiers were heading out to battle. They told him about the challenge of Goliath and how no one was brave enough to stand up to him.

Then Goliath himself came out and challenged the Israelites again. David heard him and said to his brothers, "Who is this Philistine that he should defy the armies of the living God?"

His brothers tried to send him away, but David went straight to King Saul. "I will go and fight with this Philistine for you," he said.

King Saul laughed. "You are just a boy, and he has been a great warrior for his entire life. You are not able to defeat him."

David did not waver in confidence. "As a shepherd, I defended my sheep against lions and bears. The Lord, who saved me from those beasts, will save me from the hand of this Philistine."

Not knowing what else to do, the king said, "Go, and

may the Lord be with you!"

Before David left, King Saul tried to give him strong armor and a shield to defend himself and a sword to fight, but they were too heavy for the boy. Instead, David took his staff and chose five smooth stones to use with his sling.

As David approached, Goliath cursed him and said, "Am I a dog, that you come to me with sticks?"

"You come to me with sword and spear, but I come to you in the name of the Lord of hosts, the God of the armies of Israel," David shouted in reply.

Goliath walked toward David with weapons raised, and David charged at the warrior to meet him. He drew out of his bag a stone and used his sling to hit Goliath in the forehead. The warrior fell face-first into the ground with a thud. David took Goliath's sword and killed the warrior before he could stand up again.

The Philistines fled and the Israelites were victorious, all thanks to David's great faith in God.

REFLECTION QUESTIONS

Why did David have the confidence to defeat Goliath when everyone else in the army was afraid to face him?

How has God helped you in difficult times like he did for David as a shepherd and in his battle with Goliath?

What are some things that cause you to be afraid, and how can you turn to God for confidence like David?

ELIJAH AND THE WIDOW OF ZAREPHATH

1 Kings 17:8–24

Immediately after the prophet Elijah appears for the first time in the Bible, he is sent by God to a widow living in the city of Zarephath. She was not one of the Israelites, yet God sent Elijah to her during a very difficult time.

As you read this story, pay attention to the miracles God performs for the widow through the Prophet Elijah.

God called Elijah to become his prophet during a great famine in the land of Israel. God told him, "Go now to Zarephath and live there. I have commanded a widow there to feed you."

So Elijah set out for the city. When he arrived there, he saw a woman outside the gate gathering sticks. He knew this must be the widow that God had told him to find.

"Bring me some of your bread," he said to her.

The woman looked at him in sadness. "As the Lord

your God lives, I have no bread prepared. I have only a small portion of crumbs in a jar and a little oil to go with it. I am gathering sticks for a small fire to prepare a last meal for me and my son. After that, we will die of hunger."

"Do not be afraid," Elijah said to her. "Go and make your meal, but first make me a little cake of bread. Then afterward, you can make something for you and your son."

This surprised the woman, who knew she did not have enough to make food for all of them. Recognizing the doubt in her eyes, Elijah said, "Thus says the Lord, the God of Israel: your jar of meal will not be emptied, and the oil will not run out, until the day that this famine is over."

The woman returned to her house and was amazed to find enough meal in her jar and oil in the jug to feed them for many days. Just as Elijah said, the jar and jug did not run out.

But the woman's troubles were not at an end. Her son became sick. He was so sick that he could no longer breathe. The boy was dead, and his mother wept in sorrow.

"What have you against me, O man of God? Have you come here to cause the death of my son?" she said to Elijah.

Elijah picked up the boy and laid him in his bed. He cried out to the Lord, "O Lord my God, have you brought disaster even to this widow to whom you have sent me? Have you killed her son?"

Then Elijah hugged the body of the boy three times and prayed again, "O Lord my God, let this child's life come into him again!"

The Lord listened to the prayer of Elijah. Life came into the boy again, and he breathed easily.

Elijah took the boy back to his mother to show her the miracle God had performed. "See, your son is alive."

She said, "Now I know that you are a man of God and that the word of the Lord you speak is truth."

God had worked two miracles through Elijah, and gave hope to the woman and all the people she told about these events.

REFLECTION QUESTIONS

What miracles did God provide through Elijah for the woman, even though she wasn't an Israelite?

Who do you know that is sick and in need of your prayers, just like Elijah prayed for the widow's son?

How can we have more confidence that God can heal those people we offer up to him in prayer?

ISAIAH'S MESSAGE OF HOPE

2 Kings 18-19; Isaiah 7:13-14

During King Hezekiah's reign over the Kingdom of Judah and while Isaiah was a prophet, the Assyrians came with armies to conquer God's people. First they conquered the northern Kingdom of Israel; then they moved on to conquer Judah and the great city of Jerusalem, the place of God's Temple.

As you read this story, pay attention to why God protects the city of Jerusalem.

The Assyrian army arrived outside the gates of Jerusalem. The Assyrian emissary announced to the people of Judah, "Thus says the great king of Assyria: on whom do you rely in opposition against me? Your God? Your king? Ha! Do not let Hezekiah your king deceive you. Your God will not protect you."

The people were silent, for King Hezekiah had told them not to respond.

The king was faithful to God. He went to the Temple

and prayed, "O Lord, the God of Israel, who is enthroned above the great angels, you are God, you alone over all the kingdoms of the earth. You have made heaven and earth. Listen to the words of the Assyrians, who make jokes about you. They have conquered so many lands, and now they approach us. O Lord our God, save us, I pray to you, from the hand of the Assyrians, so that all the kingdoms of the earth may know that you, O Lord, are God alone."

The prophet Isaiah heard Hezekiah's prayer. He came to the king and proclaimed, "Thus says the Lord, the God of Israel: I have heard your prayer to me about the Assyrians. They have mocked the Lord! I know when they sit and when they stand. I know when they come and when they go. I have heard their arrogance. I will turn them back the way they came!"

The Kingdom of Judah was protected, at least that time. The Assyrian armies were attacked by an angel in the night, and they fled back to their land.

Years later, after King Hezekiah died, his son lost faith in the Lord. He set up places to worship other gods, and the people went there to offer their prayers. Because they abandoned the Lord, the city of Jerusalem was eventually overtaken by the Assyrians.

Still, the people remembered a prophecy of Isaiah from a time when King Hezekiah's father reigned: "Listen, O house of David! The Lord will give you a sign: the virgin shall be with child and shall bear a son and name him Immanuel, which means 'God is with us!'"

REFLECTION QUESTIONS

What did King Hezekiah do before the Lord came to protect the city of Jerusalem?

What can you bring to the Lord in prayer to ask for his help and protection?

Why did the city of Jerusalem and the Kingdom of Judah ultimately fall to the Assyrians?

How does knowing that Jesus Christ is with you give you hope during difficult times?

THE ANNUNCIATION

Luke 1:26–38

The virgin whom Isaiah spoke of in his prophecy about the coming of the Messiah was a young woman named Mary in Galilee, who was set to marry a man named Joseph. An angel appeared to Mary to announce the birth of her son, and her reaction provides for us a wonderful example of faith.

As you read this story, pay attention to the way the Virgin Mary responds to the words of the angel Gabriel.

The angel Gabriel appeared to the Virgin Mary, saying, "Hail, favored one! The Lord is with you."

Mary was confused by the angel's words and wondered what he meant by this.

The angel said to her, "Do not be afraid, Mary, for you have found favor with God. Behold, you will conceive in your womb and bear a son, and you will name him Jesus. He will be great and will be called the Son of the

Most High. He will be a king, and his kingdom will have no end."

Mary said to the angel, "How can this be, since I am still unmarried and a virgin?"

The angel replied, "The Holy Spirit will come upon you, and the power of the Most High will overshadow you. The child to be born will be holy. He will be called Son of God."

As if to erase any other doubt, the angel continued, "Your cousin Elizabeth has also conceived a son in her old age. She is already six months pregnant. For nothing will be impossible with God."

Mary responded with an act of humble faith in God's will. She said, "Behold, I am the handmaid of the Lord. May it be done to me according to your word."

It was an awesome responsibility, and both Mary and her husband Joseph placed their trust in the Lord to give them the strength to do his will.

REFLECTION QUESTIONS

How did Mary react to the words of the angel?

How would you react if you were Mary?

In what ways can we become handmaids (or servants) of the Lord?

In what areas of your life do you need to trust in God more and let things be done according to his will and not yours?

THE BIRTH OF JESUS

Luke 2:1-19

Mary and her husband Joseph had to return to their hometown of Bethlehem. Jesus was about to be born at any time, but they still needed to go, according to the order of the Roman emperor.

As you read this story, pay attention to the message that the angel brings to the shepherds near Bethlehem.

Joseph and Mary arrived in Bethlehem, but there was no room for them in the inn. The only place left for them was a stable in the farm behind the inn.

Mary gave birth to her son, and they named him Jesus. She wrapped him in swaddling clothes and laid him in a manger that animals had used to eat out of before they arrived.

Not far from Bethlehem, there were shepherds in a field watching over their sheep. Suddenly, an angel of the Lord appeared to them in glory. The shepherds were struck with fear.

"Do not be afraid," the angel said to them. "Behold, I bring you good news of great joy for all the world. To you this day is born in Bethlehem a Savior, who is the Messiah, the Lord. You will find him wrapped in swaddling clothes and lying in a manger."

Then the shepherds saw many, many angels appear, praising God, saying, "Glory to God in the highest, and on earth, peace to those on whom his favor rests!"

The angels left them, and the shepherds went as fast as they could to find Mary and Joseph and the baby lying in the manger. The shepherds told the new parents all that the angels had said about the child. Mary and Joseph were amazed.

Mary would treasure all that she heard and think deeply about the shepherds' words in her heart in the years to come. The shepherds went away glorifying and praising God for all that they had seen and heard. As the angel said, this is good news for the whole world. There were many people that needed to hear this message of hope.

REFLECTION QUESTIONS

What message did the angel bring to the shepherds?

In what ways does Jesus bring peace into our world today?

How can we, like Mary, think deeply about this and other stories from the Bible?

JESUS HEALS THE LEPER

Matthew 8:1–4; Mark 1:40–45; Luke 5:12–15

There were many diseases in the ancient world without cures yet. Leprosy was a disease that caused someone's skin to break out in large bumps. It was very contagious, so anyone with leprosy was sent away from the communities to live in isolation.

As you read this story, pay attention to what Jesus says and does when he heals the man with leprosy.

Jesus came down from a mountain after teaching the crowds of people that followed him. Then a man with leprosy came forward. Jesus's disciples and those around him were anxious. They were afraid of getting sick, too.

The leper said, "Lord, if you choose, you can make me clean."

Jesus felt pity for the leper. He reached out his hand to touch him and said, "I do choose. Be made clean!"

Immediately, the man's skin changed and he was healed. The leprosy was gone!

Jesus told the man to go and show himself to a priest for inspection so that he would be allowed back into the community.

He also warned him not to say anything to anyone, but the man couldn't keep the story of this miracle to himself. He told everyone about the miracle. People started to come from all over to seek out Jesus to be healed, as well.

REFLECTION QUESTIONS

What did Jesus do to make the leper feel loved while everyone else was afraid of getting sick?

Who do you know that needs prayers for Jesus's healing touch?

What are some miracles or other stories you can share with people about Jesus?

JESUS HEALS THE CANAANITE WOMAN'S DAUGHTER

Matthew 15:21–28; Mark 7:24–30

Jesus was one of the people of Israel. They were called the Jews, and they were God's people. The Gentiles were people who were not Jewish. The Jews expected a Messiah to help and save them and to restore their kingdom. They did not think this applied to the Gentiles. But God had a different plan.

As you read this story, pay attention to the reason Jesus finally heals the Canaanite woman's daughter.

Jesus and his disciples traveled to a place where mostly Gentiles lived. A Canaanite woman from the area saw them and shouted to Jesus, "Have mercy on me, Lord, Son of David! My daughter is tormented by a demon."

At first Jesus did not answer her, but she kept shouting after him, hoping he would agree to heal her daughter.

Jesus's disciples said to him, "Send her away. She keeps shouting at us."

Jesus answered, "I was sent only to the lost sheep of the house of Israel."

Still, the woman persisted. She ran up to Jesus and knelt down before him. "Lord, help me," she said.

"Is it fair to take the food of children and throw it to the dogs?" he said. By this he meant that he was sent first to the people of Israel, while she was one of the Gentiles, who were not Jewish.

"But Lord, even the dogs eat the crumbs that fall from their master's table," she replied humbly.

Jesus answered, "Woman, great is your faith! Let it be done for you as you wish."

Her daughter was healed at that moment.

REFLECTION QUESTIONS

Why did Jesus heal the woman's daughter?

Who do you think feels like the Gentile woman today? Who are the people who do not go to church with you that might need healing?

How can we be as persistent in prayer as the woman was in this story?

JESUS HEALS BLIND BARTIMAEUS

Mark 10:46–52

Jesus healed many people who were blind in the Bible. The blind were often begging for money, because their lack of sight made it impossible for them to find work.

As you read this story, pay attention to the way Bartimaeus shows he has strong faith in Jesus.

Jesus and his disciples were leaving the city of Jericho, with a large crowd of people following behind them. As they left the city, a blind beggar named Bartimaeus sat on the side of the road.

"Jesus of Nazareth is coming this way," the beggar heard someone say nearby.

When Bartimaeus heard this, he shouted out, "Jesus, Son of David, have mercy on me!"

"Be quiet!" said the people nearby. But the blind man shouted even louder, "Son of David, have mercy on me!"

Jesus heard the man and stood still. "Call him here," he said.

The people called the blind man over, saying, "Take heart; get up, he is calling you."

Bartimaeus sprang up and left his cloak behind as he made his way toward Jesus.

"What do you want me to do for you?" Jesus asked Bartimaeus.

"My teacher, let me see again," he replied.

"Go," Jesus said. "Your faith has made you well."

Suddenly, Bartimaeus could see again. He jumped with joy, and tears came streaming down his face.

Jesus continued along the road with the crowd and his disciples. Bartimaeus followed him along the way toward Jerusalem, rejoicing at his newfound sight.

REFLECTION QUESTIONS

How did Bartimaeus show courage and faith?

Imagine if Jesus asked you the same question he asked Bartimaeus: "What do you want me to do for you?" What would you say in response?

JESUS HEALS THE CENTURION'S SERVANT

Matthew 8:5–13

The Romans ruled over the land of Israel during the time of Jesus. There were many Roman soldiers stationed there. These Romans worshipped Roman gods, yet the centurion in this story had faith in Jesus Christ.

As you read this story, pay attention to the faith that the centurion shows in Jesus, even though he is not Jewish or one of Jesus's followers.

As Jesus entered Capernaum, a Roman centurion approached him, pleading for help. Centurions were commanders of one hundred soldiers in the Roman army.

"Lord, my servant is lying at home, paralyzed and in terrible distress," he said.

Jesus replied, "I will come and cure him."

The centurion was surprised by the response. "Lord, I

am not worthy to have you come under my roof; but only speak the word, and my servant will be healed."

Jesus was amazed by the centurion's words. "Truly, I tell you, in no one in Israel have I found such faith. Many will come from outside of Israel to eat with Abraham and Isaac and Jacob in the kingdom of heaven, while those who reject me will be thrown into darkness."

Jesus turned to the centurion and said, "Go; let it be done for you according to your faith."

The centurion's servant was healed in that hour.

REFLECTION QUESTIONS

How did the Roman centurion show his faith in Jesus?

How can we strengthen our faith and humility before Jesus like the centurion in the story?

In what ways do you or people you know need the healing power of Jesus?

JESUS CALMS THE STORM

Matthew 8:23-27; Mark 4:35-41; Luke 8:22-25

Jesus traveled around all of Israel, preaching to crowds of people and healing their sick. With him he brought a small group of disciples that he taught separately from the crowds. He often taught them lessons about faith in unexpected ways.

As you read this story, pay attention to the lesson Jesus gives to the disciples in their moment of fear.

After Jesus had taught large crowds of people one day, he said to his disciples, "Let us get into this boat and travel to the other side of the lake."

The disciples got into the boat and set out into the water. Jesus lay down in the front of the boat and fell asleep.

Suddenly, a storm came upon them. The wind blew harder and harder until the boat was filling up with water.

Jesus continued to sleep through the storm. The disciples tried to wake him. They were very afraid. "Lord, save us! We are going to drown!"

Jesus woke up and stood before the blowing wind and crashing waves. He raised a hand toward the sea and said, "Peace! Be still!"

The wind died down, and the waters became calm again. Jesus turned toward his disciples.

"Why are you afraid? Where is your faith?" he asked them.

The disciples were amazed and said to each other, "What sort of man is this, that even the wind and the sea obey him?"

REFLECTION QUESTIONS

Why did Jesus question the disciples for being afraid? What did he expect from them instead?

When times feel chaotic and out of control, how can you practice faith that Jesus will calm the storm?

Who do you know that needs comfort and peace right now? How can you help calm their storm?

Imagine Jesus saying the words "peace" and "be still" to you. How would this make you feel?

PARABLE OF THE LOST SHEEP

Luke 15:1–7

The lessons in Jesus's parables were always unexpected. Jesus told these stories to show people how much God loves even those who are struggling in life. In this parable, Jesus explains how God is like a shepherd who searches for even one lost sheep.

As you read this story, pay attention to the lesson Jesus gives to explain this parable.

Many of the people listening to Jesus preach were tax collectors and others who were known to be sinful people. The scribes and Pharisees, who were supposed to be holy men, grumbled about Jesus spending his time with sinners. So Jesus told them a parable about a shepherd and a lost sheep.

He said that a shepherd cared for a flock of one hundred sheep in the fields. Then one day the shepherd noticed that one of his sheep was missing. It was lost!

So the shepherd left the ninety-nine sheep all alone to go searching for the one that was lost. He searched for a long time, until he finally found it.

The shepherd shouted with joy, and then he lifted up the lost sheep and placed it on his shoulders. He carried the lost sheep on his back until he returned to his home. He went out and found his friends. Then he knocked on his neighbors' doors to wake them up. He proclaimed to them, "Rejoice with me, for I have found my lost sheep!"

When Jesus finished his story, he said to the tax collectors, sinners, scribes, and Pharisees: "In the same way, there will be more joy in heaven over one sinner who turns back to God than over the ninety-nine good people who are already with God."

REFLECTION QUESTIONS

Why would the shepherd leave the ninety-nine remaining sheep to go searching for the one that was lost?

What would it feel like to be the lost sheep that the shepherd came to find?

When we are one of the ninety-nine good people who are with God, how can we prayerfully support the ones that are lost?

THE PRODIGAL SON RETURNS

Luke 15:11–32

Jesus told a story that we know as the Parable of the Prodigal Son. It is about a young son who wasted his share of his father's property. The father in the parable is God our Father. The son in the story is a person who sins but then seeks God's forgiveness.

As you read this story, pay attention to the way the father receives his returning sinful son.

A man had two sons. Normally, a father would pass on his money and property to his sons after his death, but the younger son asked his father to give him his share early.

The younger son took all this money and traveled far away. He wasted it all, until he had nothing left. He was poor and hungry.

He went to a farmer and asked him for a job. The farmer sent him to take care of the pigs. Even the pigs ate better food than the young son was able to eat. The son realized his mistake. He had lost everything. He was alone and hungry and without any hope that he could make things right on his own.

He decided he had to go home. There he would ask his father to hire him as a servant. He did not want any special treatment as his son. He was certain that his father would be angry with him if he came back.

When he returned home, however, his father saw him from a distance. He ran from the house toward his son. He hugged him with all his might, and tears of joy filled his eyes.

Then the young man said, "Father, I have sinned against heaven and against you. I no longer deserve to be called your son. Treat me as you would treat one of your hired workers."

The father continued his joyful acceptance of the son's return. Instead of punishing him, he threw a big party to welcome the son home, because his son had been lost, but now he was back home.

REFLECTION QUESTIONS

What did the father do when he saw his son return?

In what ways do you think God comes running to forgive and embrace us when we return after our sin?

What would you say to someone who felt too ashamed to pray to God or go to church?

THE PARABLE OF THE GOOD SAMARITAN

Luke 10:25–37

The Jews did not like the Samaritans. The Samaritans did not worship God in Jerusalem like the Jews did. So they avoided the Samaritans at all costs. For this reason, the parable of the Good Samaritan was a surprise to those who heard it.

As you read this story, pay attention to the way the Samaritan is a good neighbor.

A lawyer came up to Jesus and asked, "What must I do to get to heaven?"

Jesus asked him, "What is written in the law?"

"You shall love God, and love your neighbor as yourself," the lawyer replied.

"You are correct. Do this, and you will live forever," he told him.

"Okay, but who is my neighbor?" the lawyer asked Jesus.

In response, Jesus told him and the people there a parable.

He said that there was a man walking from Jerusalem to Jericho. Robbers attacked the man and beat him up and stole everything he had. They left him nearly dead.

A priest was walking up the road when he saw the bloody man. The priest walked around the man on the other side of the road to avoid him.

Then a Levite, who was also supposed to be a holy man as someone who helped in the Temple, saw the bloody man in the road. He, too, avoided him, passing by on the other side.

Then a Samaritan man approached. When he saw the bloody Jewish man, he was moved with pity. He ran to him and bandaged his wounds and treated him with care. He picked up the man and placed him on his horse. He took the man to an inn and rented a room to take care of him overnight.

The next day, he went to the innkeeper and gave him two days' wages. He said, "Take care of the man. He is very hurt. I must go and finish some business, but when I return, I will repay you whatever you spend to care for him."

When Jesus finished the parable, he said to the lawyer, "Which of these three—the priest, the Levite, or the Samaritan—was a neighbor to the man who was robbed?"

The lawyer said, "The one who showed him mercy."

Jesus replied, "Go and do likewise for your neighbors."

REFLECTION QUESTIONS

What did the Samaritan do as a good neighbor for the man?

How can you be a good neighbor to people who are bullied at school?

How can you give hope to someone who is struggling and alone?

THE RAISING OF LAZARUS

John 11

The shortest verse in the Bible is a two-word sentence: "Jesus wept" (John 11:35; sometimes the verse is translated as "Jesus began to weep"). Jesus cried when he learned of his friend Lazarus's death, but the story does not end there. He brought his friend back to life!

As you read this story, pay attention to the reaction Jesus had when he saw the people crying.

Jesus received a message from his friends Martha and Mary, who lived in Bethany in Judea. They said that their brother, Lazarus, was ill. The sisters seemed very afraid, but Jesus was confident that God would be glorified through this illness.

He told his disciples they would go back to Judea, even though people there wanted to kill him. "Our friend Lazarus has fallen asleep, but I am going there to awaken him," he told his disciples.

"Lord, if he has only fallen asleep, then he will be just

fine," they replied.

Jesus said very plainly, "Lazarus is dead. For your sake, I am glad I was not there, so that you may believe. Let us go to him now."

By the time Jesus and the disciples arrived in Bethany, Lazarus had already been in a tomb for four days. Many people were there to comfort Martha and Mary for the loss of their brother.

Martha saw Jesus coming first. "Lord, if you were here, then he would not have died," she told him.

"Your brother will rise again," Jesus replied.

"I know that he will rise again in the resurrection on the last day," Martha said sadly.

"Those who believe in me, even though they die, will live, and everyone who lives and believes in me will never die. Do you believe this?" he asked her.

"Yes, Lord, I believe that you are the Messiah, the Son of God, the one coming into the world," said Martha. Then she called her sister Mary to join them.

Mary quickly came to them. The many people who had come to comfort the sisters followed closely behind her. She knelt at Jesus's feet and said, "Lord, if you had been here, my brother would not have died."

Jesus saw her weeping. The people wept with Mary, too. He was greatly moved.

"Where have you laid him?" Jesus asked.

"Lord, come and see," they said.

Then, Jesus wept.

"See how he loved him!" the people said. "If only he had been here to stop this man from dying."

Jesus came to the tomb and stood outside the entrance to the cave, where a stone was laid against it. "Take away the stone," he said.

They took away the stone, and Jesus looked up to heaven and prayed, "Father, I thank you for having heard me. I know that you always hear me, but I have said this for the sake of the crowd standing here, so that they may believe that you sent me."

Then he shouted, "Lazarus, come out!"

To the amazement of everyone there, Lazarus emerged from the tomb, with his face, hands, and feet still bound in burial cloths.

His sisters were filled with joy. Many people there came to believe in Jesus on that day. They rejoiced, because Lazarus was alive again!

REFLECTION QUESTIONS

Why do you think Jesus wept?

When someone loses a loved one, how can you comfort them in their sorrow?

Do you ever think about Jesus weeping with you when you are sad?

CRIMINALS ON THE CROSS

Luke 23:32, 39–40

Jesus was not crucified alone. There were criminals there with him who were also sentenced to death. This is the story of a conversation Jesus had with the two other men who were crucified by his side.

As you read this story, pay attention to what Jesus promises to the criminal who defends him.

The soldiers nailed Jesus's hands and feet to the cross and raised it high. Two criminals were also nailed to crosses on his right and left.

One of the criminals said, "Are you not the Messiah? Save yourself and us!"

But the other criminal scolded the man. "Do you not fear God? You are condemned to death just like us, but you and I are getting what we deserve. This man has done nothing wrong."

He looked to Jesus and said, "Jesus, remember me when you come into your kingdom."

Jesus replied, "Today you will be with me in the Paradise of heaven."

REFLECTION QUESTIONS

What is the Paradise that Jesus promises to the criminal who spoke up for him?

When have you felt like either one of the criminals who were crucified with Jesus?

How can you defend Jesus to those who do not believe in him?

JESUS IS RISEN

Matthew 28:1-10; Mark 16:1-7; Luke 24:1-10; John 20:1-10

Death is very sad, but we can have great hope in everlasting life because Jesus defeated death through his resurrection. The story of Jesus does not end in the tomb. He died and rose again so that we might also die and rise with him in the Kingdom of Heaven.

As you read this story, pay attention to the message that the angels share with the women at the tomb.

On Sunday morning, the first day of the week, Mary Magdalene, Mary the mother of the apostles James and John, and a woman named Joanna went to Jesus's tomb. They were very sad and heartbroken over the loss of the Lord Jesus. On this morning, they came with spices to anoint his body.

Along the way, Mary Magdalene asked the others, "Who will roll back the stone for us from the entrance of our Lord's tomb?"

The others did not know the answer. Still, they went on their way.

As they arrived at the tomb, the sun was rising. They were astonished to see that the very large stone covering the entrance had already been rolled away.

They ran to the tomb and looked inside. The body of Jesus was gone!

They were shocked and confused, but then two angels wearing dazzling clothing appeared. The women were terrified. They covered their faces and looked to the ground.

"Why do you look for the living among the dead?" the angels said to them. "You seek Jesus of Nazareth. He is not here. He has been raised!"

The women's eyes filled with tears of joy. They suddenly remembered that Jesus said the Son of Man would die and rise again on the third day.

Filled with joy, they rushed away from the tomb to tell the other disciples all that they had seen and heard. They could hardly contain their excitement as they went on their way.

REFLECTION QUESTIONS

What message did the angels give to the women at the tomb?

How can you announce to others the great gift of Jesus's death and resurrection?

THE ROAD TO EMMAUS

Luke 24:13-35

After Jesus rose from the dead, he appeared to many of his disciples. He encountered two of these disciples shortly after his death and resurrection just outside of Jerusalem. They were traveling on the road to a village called Emmaus.

As you read this story, pay attention to the way the disciples finally realize that it was Jesus who was with them.

It was a difficult few days for the disciples of Jesus. They had seen and heard about the death of their Lord. They were all alone now with no one to lead them. Two of these disciples left the city of Jerusalem, where Jesus was crucified, and began to walk the seven miles to a village called Emmaus.

They were walking along the road, talking about all that had happened, when Jesus came near and began to walk with them. In their sadness, the disciples did not recognize that it was Jesus who came near to them.

"What are you talking about as you walk along the road?" Jesus asked.

They stopped and looked at one another in sadness. "Are you the only one in Jerusalem who does not know the things that have taken place these last few days?"

"What things?" Jesus asked.

"The things about Jesus of Nazareth, and how our chief priests and leaders handed him over to be crucified," said one of the disciples.

"We had hoped that he was the one who would redeem Israel. Today is the third day since he died," said the other disciple.

The first disciple jumped in and said, "Moreover, some women of our group have astounded us. They were at his tomb this morning, and they did not find his body there. They told us they had a vision of angels who said he was alive!"

"Others went to the tomb and found it just as the women had said, but they did not see him," said the other disciple.

"Oh, how foolish you are, and slow of heart to believe all that the prophets declared!" Jesus said. "It was necessary that the Messiah should suffer these things and enter into his glory."

Then, as they continued to walk, Jesus interpreted

many things that the prophets, beginning with Moses, had said about him in the scriptures.

Finally, they arrived in the village of Emmaus, and Jesus walked ahead of them.

"Stay with us! It is almost evening, and the day is now nearly over," the disciples shouted.

So Jesus came back to stay with them. They sat down for a meal, and Jesus took bread, blessed and broke it, and gave it to the disciples.

At that moment, their eyes were opened, and they recognized Jesus for the first time. Then he vanished from their sight.

They turned to each other. "Were not our hearts burning within us while he was explaining the scriptures to us?"

They got up immediately and returned to Jerusalem to tell the apostles about their encounter with Christ.

REFLECTION QUESTIONS

When did the disciples finally recognize Jesus?

Who helps you understand the scriptures?

How can going to church help you experience God's love in times of trouble?

JESUS GIVES THE HOLY SPIRIT

John 20:19–23

When Jesus was arrested, the disciples scattered and fled in fear. After he died, though, they gathered back together again in sadness. Still, they were afraid for their lives. They started to have doubts that Jesus would rise again, until finally, he appeared to them.

As you read this story, pay attention to how Jesus greets the fearful disciples.

On the third day after Jesus died, the disciples gathered together behind locked doors. They were hiding for fear of the Jews that had killed Jesus. They were sad and afraid.

Suddenly, Jesus appeared in the middle of the room. "Peace be with you," he said to them.

The disciples were amazed. They thought Jesus was dead, yet here he stood among them. Some of them had doubt that it truly was Jesus, so the Lord showed them the wounds in his hands and in his side.

When they saw that it was Jesus, the disciples rejoiced! Their Lord was alive! He was risen!

Jesus said to them again, "Peace be with you. As the Father has sent me, so I send you."

Then Jesus did something quite unexpected. He opened his mouth and breathed on them. "Receive the Holy Spirit. If you forgive someone's sins, they will be forgiven."

The Holy Spirit took away their fear. Jesus gave them peace and the power to share that peace with the whole world.

REFLECTION QUESTIONS

How did Jesus greet the sad and fearful disciples?

What fears do you have right now that you can offer up to the Lord, seeking his Holy Spirit to comfort you?

How can you bring the gift of peace in the world today?

THE ASCENSION

After his resurrection, Jesus remained with the disciples for forty days. Eventually, it was time for him to return to his Father in heaven, but not before giving his followers a few parting words of hope.

As you read this story, pay attention to the reasons the apostles are filled with hope instead of fear after Jesus ascends up into heaven.

Jesus gathered his disciples together and they asked him, "Lord, are you going to restore the Kingdom of Israel now?"

Jesus was staring up into the sky. He looked to his disciples and replied, "It is not for you to know the time that the Father has planned for his kingdom. But you will receive power when the Holy Spirit has come upon you; and you will be my witnesses in Jerusalem, in all Judea and Samaria, and to the ends of the earth."

Then, to the amazement of the disciples, Jesus began

to float up into the air. He rose higher and higher into the clouds until they could see him no more.

They were staring up into the sky when two men in white robes appeared by their sides. They were angels. They said, "Why do you stand looking up toward heaven? This Jesus, who has ascended into heaven, will come in the same way as you saw him go into heaven."

The angels left them, and the men returned to Jerusalem. As they walked along the way, they remembered some parting words Jesus had spoken to them not long before. He told them, "Go and make disciples of all nations, baptizing them in the name of the Father and of the Son and of the Holy Spirit, and teaching them to obey everything that I have commanded you. And remember, I am with you always, to the end of the age."

With a renewed sense of hope in the future, the apostles began their mission to make more disciples of Christ throughout the world.

REFLECTION QUESTIONS

What did Jesus tell the apostles to do after he left?

Why do you think the apostles felt hope after Jesus ascended up into heaven?

How can you be Jesus Christ's witness and teach others about what he said and did?

ABOUT BIBLE BREAKS

The Bible Breaks stories for kids help families and faith formation groups set aside a few minutes during the day to read and reflect on the Word of God. Each short and simple story is written to help teach children the most important lessons of the Christian life from sacred Scripture.

Learn more at jareddees.com/biblebreaks

ABOUT THE AUTHOR

Jared Dees is the creator of *TheReligionTeacher.com*, a popular website that provides practical resources and teaching strategies to religious educators. A respected graduate of the Alliance for Catholic Education (ACE) program at the University of Notre Dame, Dees holds master's degrees in education and theology, both from Notre Dame. He frequently gives keynotes and leads workshops at conferences, church events, and school in-services throughout the year on a variety of topics. He lives near South Bend, Indiana, with his wife and children.

Learn more about Jared's books, speaking events, and other projects at jareddees.com.

amazon.com/author/jareddees
facebook.com/jareddeesauthor
instagram.com/jareddees
twitter.com/jareddees
youtube.com/thereligionteacher

ALSO BY JARED DEES

Jared Dees is the author of numerous books, including a short story collection titled *Beatitales: 80 Fables about the Beatitudes for Children*.

Download a collection of these stories at jareddees.com/beatitales.

BOOKS BY JARED DEES

31 Days to Becoming a Better Religious Educator

To Heal, Proclaim, and Teach

Praying the Angelus

Christ in the Classroom

Beatitales

Tales of the Ten Commandments

Made in the USA
Columbia, SC
27 May 2020